THE

KIDDIEPRENEUR

IN YOU

Chrissy Steed

Copyright © 2015

Disclaimer

Dedication

I would like to thank GOD who continues to guide my every move and for loving me unconditionally. I dedicate this book to my loving daughter Amiya Steed who is my 1st KiddiePreneur with her own clothing line Amiya Baby Collections. Please believe that through God, determination and passion all things are possible. Mommy loves you very much.

My family is an everlasting support to me, especially my parents Sue and Michael Sr., step-parents – Shanette and Tony, sisters – Carolyn, Michelle and in heaven Nicole, brothers – Michael and Dwight, nieces Jalah, Ayanna, Morgan and Nicole and nephews – Malachi, Isaiah and Elijah. There are a few people who assisted me with this book and deserve a special acknowledgement; Royal Graphix my brother Michael's photography company captured these great photos that you see throughout the book and my sister Carolyn for her expert graphic designing skills and producing my great book cover.

Thank you to my friend/sister Tara, all conferences/expos who have graciously invited me to speak at their events and to everyone who continues to support the Just 4 U Kids and KiddiePreneur nationwide movement. Enjoy the book and I can't wait to see the explosion of KiddiePreneurs throughout the world.

Be sure to register your child for our KiddiePreneur Online Training Academy at www.KiddiePreneur.com

Blessings,
Chrissy Steed, MBA

My Story

So you're interested in becoming a KiddiePreneur? You are a hard worker and are extremely **determined.** You have a **great idea.** You just need a little **help.**

When I was younger, I was just like you! I had a plan to make a difference and leave my footprint on the world. I was **only 14 years old** and I was a KiddiePreneur.

I loved to perform and used my passion to help other kids learn to perform. I founded my own community dance and performing arts program for inner-city kids. What a huge success it ended up being! I turned my hobby and passion into a business that lasted for several years.

I was soooooooooo excited about my business that making money never crossed my mind. I was helping others! As a KiddiePreneur you too can make money doing what you love!

Table of Contents

What Is a KiddiePreneur?

✅ A kid who likes to figure out **new ways** of doing things, even if it's risky.

Risky means it's not the safest. You're taking a chance!

✅ A kid who knows when they have a good idea and is **determined** to make it work.

✅ A kid who thinks of new and better ways **to do things.**

✅ A kid who **knows** they can't do it alone, but still wants to succeed.

☑ A kid who cannot be stopped once an idea is in their head!

Is It For Me?

Sometimes kids hear the word "business" and think "boring." But business can be more exciting than you think. Talk with loved ones about it and you'll see! Business is just finding a way to succeed at something you love. What's cooler than that?

Think of business as getting ready for your future. Your future should excite you. It should make you want to accomplish things and to find creative ways to reach your goals. Every move you make in life is a way of building the path towards your goal.

What do you find fun? Let me guess... Video games. Amusement parks. Friends. Sports. TV. Going on the computer. Yes, you're right, those things are fun. But the right business can be fun too.

Know what the best part is? You'll be winning! If you succeed at your goal, make money doing it, and can earn a living for yourself, that is really the grand prize in life. You're making your ideas come true!

But beware! Business is not for those that will give up when things get hard. It will be a lot of work. There will be hard days. There will be times that you will miss parties or your favorite TV show. Just remember... YOU GET WHAT YOU PUT IN! If you put time and energy into your business, you will be rewarded.

The Plan

This is the hardest part of being a **KiddiePreneur,** but it's how every business starts. When you think about how you are going to make your idea come true, you make what is called a **business plan.** This helps you focus on the far-away future, not just on next week or next month.

Business plans can be overwhelming. You might have a great plan, but you're just a kid afterall, right? Well, this is half true. There is a lot that might be hard to **understand** and you will want a grown up to help you. This is fine, but you should still get involved. It will help you be a better **KiddiePreneur** and even help you make your idea better. Even if it seems like a lot and you are feeling like this is "grown-up work," just remember... The more you try to be a part of it, the more experience you will have and the easier this will all become.

So, here's what you do:

Describe It: You have to be able to explain your idea. Write a few sentences that tell what your idea is and what your plan is. Don't make it too long, but also make sure that it is easy to understand.

Get More People: You can't do this alone. Even grown-ups have a team that helps them start a business. Write down who is going to help you and why they are the best person for the job. And add yourself to the list! You can get silly with this and even explain how having to clean your room every week makes you a great **business person!**

Picture It: Make sure you have a very clear picture in your head. What are you naming your product or idea? Who are you **planning** on selling this to? Is this something people will need or want? How will you **convince** them to buy it? This will be your vision for your business.

Stop the Problems: Plan ahead for problems, so that you have the solutions ready to go. What if another kid tries to steal your idea and sell it first? Are you trying to sell it to the right people? You wouldn't set up a **lemonade stand** in an empty parking lot, because no one would come. You would set it up in your front yard or at the corner where cars pass by. Think about every detail.

Make It Unique: This can be tough. It is like when your teacher tells you to start your writing with a "hook" to grab the reader's attention. Except you have to grab the buyer's attention! Why is your idea so special? What is so awesome about what you are doing or planning?

Stand Out: When starting a business, you are not going to be successful if you try to sell something that is already being sold. Your idea needs to stand out. Think about, and even write down, who your competition would be and why your idea is better. Is your idea totally new? Did someone else start this idea years ago, but you have found a way to make it better?

Spread the Word: Plan out how you will spread the word and let people know about your business. Ads in the newspaper, flyers, calling people, social media, posters at the grocery store... What's your plan for **letting everyone** know your business has arrived and that they **must patronize** your business? Also, ask your family members and friends to help you spread the word about your business. You will be **surprised** by how many people will jump at the opportunity to help you spread the word about your business for **FREE!**

Money, Money, Money: You don't have to have all the money you need right from the start, but you need a plan for how you are going to get it. You can have fundraisers or ask for donations. First, however, you need to plan how much you will need, so that you know what your fundraising goal is.

MISSION STATEMENT

The best example of a **mission statement** will define a company and its purpose in 30 seconds or less. This is an eloquent, **concise paragraph** that should be full of meaning and impact. Choose your words wisely- beware of buzz words, empty phrases, or mission statements that are so general they could **apply** to many different companies. It's a **challenge,** but you want to capture what your company stands for in a brief and memorable way.

With your **mission statement,** you should be sure to cover what the goals of your business are for these three primary components essential to the viability of a KiddiePreneur business: customers, employees, and owners. Be clear and specific, and you'll highlight the core of what makes your venture unique and worthwhile.

To test the value of a draft of your mission statement, take a step back and ask yourself whether or not the same words could apply to any other business; and whether anybody could immediately identify your KiddiePreneur business from hearing your mission statement.

VISION STATEMENT

A **carefully crafted** and focused vision statement can and will help you communicate your **company's goals** to employees and management in a single sentence or a few concise paragraphs. While a well-thought-out statement may take a **few days or weeks** to craft, the result will be a tool that helps inspire strategic decision **making and product development** for your KiddiePreneur business for years to come.

Failure to fully understand your company's position can lead to poor decision making at all levels of an organization. For that reason, the first step towards thoughtfully **crafting a vision statement** is to take a careful look at where you are as a company, your place in the industry and your realistic goals for the intermediate and long term.

Vision statements lay out the most important primary goals and the basis for a company. Unlike business plans, vision statements generally don't outline a plan to achieve those goals. But, by outlining the key objectives for a company, vision statements enable the company's employees to develop business strategies to achieve the stated goals. With a single unifying vision statement, employees are all on the same page and can be more focused and productive.

Comparison Chart

	MISSION STATEMENT	**VISION STATEMENT**
About	A Mission statement talks about **HOW** you will get to where you want to be. Defines the purpose and primary objectives related to your customer needs and team values.	A Vision statement outlines **WHERE** you want to be. Communicates both the purpose and values of your business.
Answer	It answers the question, "What do we do? What	It answers the question, "Where do we aim to be?"

	MISSION STATEMENT	VISION STATEMENT
	makes us different?"	
Time	A mission statement talks about the present leading to its future.	A vision statement talks about your future.
Function	It lists the broad goals for which the organization is formed. To define the key measure or measures of the organization's success and its prime	It lists where you see yourself some years from now. It inspires you to give your best. It shapes your understanding of why you are working here.

	MISSION STATEMENT	**VISION STATEMENT**
	audience is the leadership, team and stockholders.	
Developing a statement	What do we do today? For whom do we do it? What is the benefit? In other words, Why we do what we do? What, For Whom and Why?	Where do we want to be going forward? When do we want to reach that stage? How do we want to do it?

Let's Talk About Business

There is a lot that you can learn when you read the description of a business. Here are some of the things:

- **Who's the Boss:** Is there a main president or is there a group of people that run the company? Who is in charge of making the decisions?

- **Lots of Info:** You can learn all about the history of a business. What things did they try that worked? What things did they try that failed?

- **Location, Location:** This not only lists what state a business might be in, but it gives their exact address. This way, if someone wants to talk to them about their idea, they know how to get in touch with the company.

- **What's the Big Idea:** A fancy way of saying this would be the business's philosophy. What are their thoughts about what they sell and what do they feel is most important? At the same time, what do their customers think?

- **Objectives:** This sounds like a big word, but it is a short, quick way of saying what the business's plan is. This can also include the vision statement, which is a bit different than the business plan. It focuses on what your goal is at the end.

- **We're On a Mission:** Think of it like a determined explorer setting off on an adventure. They're on a mission! Well, a mission statement is when a company says what their mission is, or what their goal or idea is. Just remember, the mission statement should only be about 30 seconds long - make it short and sweet!

When describing your business, it should start with a short summary. Think about when you need to write a report for your teacher, saying what a book was about. You are writing the main idea of your business. You also need to give information about the market you want to get into.

A market in business is like a category or group, like electronics or children's books.

KiddiePreneurs need to make sure that their information is correct. If you want to ask someone to donate money or sponsor you, then you had better be able to tell them about the market you are interested in and why you are a great fit for it! This would be a great time to have a grown-up help. Trying to research different markets might get confusing, and the information you find might be written for an adult reader.

Also, think about how you want your business to be structured. There are a few different ways to do it, but the main choice is to make it wholesale or retail. A wholesale business means that you are selling your product or idea to a company or buyer, and then they go on and sell it to the customers. A retail business means that you are the one selling right to the customer.

You will also need to decide who is in charge. Is there one main boss? Is it going to be an organization? Why are you picking those people to be in charge? Don't forget... People are going to want to know about YOU too! How did you come up with your idea? Why do you think it will be a success? Why are you the best person to start this business?

Now is the time to take a deep breath and rest for a moment! Phew! Once you have written all about your business, it is time to write about what you are selling. Think about when you read the back cover of a book to see if it sounds interesting. That's called a story blurb. Well, you need to write a blurb for your idea or product. Remember, you want to make your idea **sound new and unique!**

So you have your **business description** and your product blurb. What's next? Deals! Who doesn't **love** a good deal? If you saw two **comic books** at the store for the same price, but one of them *also* came with a **free candy bar,** which one would you pick? I'm guessing the one with a candy bar. That's the one most people would **pick.**

"How do I come up with and make a deal?" you might ask. Well, there are a few tricks that will help you get started. Remember earlier how you researched who your competition would be? Now is a good time to use that **information** to make your and your business look great. Let's say you decide to make home-made dolls to sell. Maybe other companies only sell the dolls in one outfit. What do you do? You sell the dolls with at least two outfits. BOOM! Your idea is now better than what is out there. It doesn't promise that your idea will be successful, but it certainly helps!

Also, make sure you don't run out of what you sell. A quick way to make your business look bad is to not have your product ready when someone wants to buy it. Plus, think about sales and coupons. Perhaps when someone purchases their very first home-made doll from you, you give them a discount on the second doll they purchase. Or perhaps you give a guarantee. That means you promise your product will work for a certain amount of time. For example, you say the doll won't fall apart or break for at least a year, and if it does they can get a new one for free.

Let's not forget that you are trying to sell this idea. You are going to have to talk about money at some point. When selling an idea or product for your business, you don't want to just say the price. You want to say why the price is a steal! Tell them about all the cool features they will get or how it will be so helpful to their life that it's actually priceless. If a person or company is going to give you money, they want to feel like they are winning the lottery. They might even ask you to write up why they should give money. Remember to give amazing details, but to keep it short so that you don't lose their attention or interest.

When in **doubt,** have a few strong lines that you can say. If you need to convince someone that they should donate money because your idea is worth it, then throw in a few super sentences to sell it! Here are a few examples:

- I have the **business idea** all sorted out

- It will have the best in-class **equipment**

- The product is very **unique**

- The **marketplace** is prepared for this

- It's an **explosive product** at a reasonable cost

Let's Talk About the Market

A **business breakdown** is when you talk about how much work a business does and how much money they make. If you are trying to get a business started, then knowing how much work and **money your business *will*** do will really help to sell your idea and make you look like an expert.

To look even **more awesome,** try to include these in your plan as well:

- **Who's Around You:** Is just a fancy way of saying "demographics and segmentation." However, in essence this simply means to know who your **neighbors** are. If you want to open a well-to-do **breakfast restaurant,** then you don't want to do it *right next* to another breakfast restaurant. You need to check out what things are in the area to make sure it is a good fit for your business, too.

- **Who's Your Audience:** You have already done some of this work before. Remember when you wrote down or thought about who would be buying your **product or idea?** Maybe it's for kids.

Maybe it's for anyone that loves electronics. Maybe it's for anyone with a bicycle. That's your audience.

- **Who Needs It:** You always want to be positive when selling something. If you go into a **pizza place** and the guy behind the counter says, "Well, this isn't the best pizza in the world, but I tried my best," are you really going to want to eat that pizza? Be prepared to say why your product or idea needs to be **made or sold.**

- **Who Do You Need To Beat:** Remember, that you have done this part already too. Who is your competition?

- **Who's Blocking Your Way:** This is a fancy way of saying this is "barriers to entry." All that means is to think about the different problems you might face.

- **Who Made the Rules:** There are always rules to follow, even as a grown-up. Though as a grown-up, most of the rules turn into serious laws. When **starting a business** there are certain rules to know. This would be another good time to have a grown-up help make sure that everything is being done the right way. A quick search on the famous internet can help in this area.

Remember, that you've **already** done some of this planning already. Your job now is to **make sure** you have put all those **pieces together** so you are ready to sell **your idea!**

Demographics and Segmentation

This is the part where you think about your neighbors. You need to know who is around you so that you know who your competition is and if you are in a good location. Depending on your idea, you might need to go a bit bigger than that. If you are opening one restaurant, then you are just building it in one area. So you just need to know about that area. But what if you sell something online and the whole country has access to it? Then you need to think about your "neighbors" all over the country. What that means is, any business in the country is like a neighbor, so you need to know what they sell and who the competition is.

Volume and Value

There are two really important numbers you are going to need to know. The first is how many possible clients or customers you might have. The other is an estimation of the how much the business will be worth.

Potential Buyer

A potential buyer means someone who might be buying your stuff. This starts by thinking of your audience again, or who you think will be a customer. However, your work is not done yet. If you are selling office furniture, you can't just think about if there are offices nearby that might need your product. You have to also remember your neighbors. If there

43

are two other furniture places in the **area,** then your number of **potential buyers** goes down. Even if you get a lot of people into your store, there will **always** be some people that go to the other furniture stores.

Business Value

Think about math class when your teacher asks about the value of *x* or the value of the number in the tens place. The **teacher** is asking how much it is worth. Well, you need to think about how much your **business is worth.** This is a lot harder to do than taking a look at your neighbors. **Grown-up** help here is a good idea. Depending on **your age** and math skills, calculating all these figures is **tricky work.** There are a lot of things to remember, such as how many **similar businesses** are both in your area and in the country.

However, this is also a time when you can hire someone **to survey** the area or evaluate things for you. Whether you do it, a **trusted grown-up** does it, or you **hire someone**, here are two ways to do it:

- The base up **methodology** is when you start with one small piece and work your way up to the larger parts. So maybe you start just with your business, then look into the business in your neighborhood, then **state**, and then **country.**

- The **top-down** methodology is when you start with the big pieces first and work your way down to the **smaller sections.** So maybe you look at the whole country first, then different states, then your neighborhood, until you are down to just your business.

Each of these methods involve using math to compare and combine how many companies and how many workers there are in certain fields. Figuring all of this out helps you to know if your plan sounds good or if you need to change some things around.

Target Market

You might remember that this is who you want to sell your product to. What is that person like? Do they like to buy expensive stuff? Do they like to feel like they are getting a lot of stuff for a low price? Think about every detail you might need to guide your business towards that kind of person.

Business Need

Now although very important, this part can be a little technical and I will not belabour the point. Simplistically, business leaders set goals and objectives for their enterprise, and they rally teams to work hard and deliver. These goals and objectives are business needs; they are the things the business must have or achieve to run, to be profitable, to serve effectively, and to deliver successfully to achieve its mission.

Articulating and defining business needs is a part of the activity called enterprise analysis and includes identifying and understanding the business's goals; articulating its strategic direction; and capturing any key concerns **pertaining** to the business's successes, challenges, risks, or problems.

Successfully identifying business needs requires critical thinking, analysis, and insight. Now that was a jammed packed segment of knowledge. Take a break now if you wish.

Rivalry

Have you ever **heard** grown-ups talk about sibling rivalry? That is when siblings fight or compete. Maybe a brother and sister are **fighting** over the TV remote. Maybe two brothers are both **trying** to win a diving contest. The point is, it is one versus the other. In business, you are **competing** against any business that sells something similar to your product.

So what do you do about it? Well, you can't put the other company in a headlock or give them a wedgie, like you might do to your pesky little brother. But you can certainly try to win the competition! Some people can get nasty when they do this. They will say mean things about the other company or try to make them look bad. I can't tell you what kind of business person to be. However, I can certainly give you tips on being a professional. (Basically, that means being a nice grown-up.)

You can still make yourself look better by just talking about yourself. So instead of saying, "That coffee shop is a big chain, so there's nothing special about it and you don't want to go there!"

I can say, "When you come to my coffee shop, you can get a unique cup of coffee like you have never tasted before, where we make every customer's drink special and with love." Do you see the difference? One way insulted the other business. The other way talked about how awesome your coffee shop was.

Let's Talk About the Boss

Who is doing what? That's what you need to decide. Is there **one boss** of the company? Will there be a group of people that always have to agree before making business decisions? No matter how **excited** you are about your business or how **prepared** you feel you are, you are going to have to have some help. This is the time to think about who you want **helping you** and how they should be doing that.

One important thing to **remember...** Don't just hire someone for your business because **you feel bad** or feel like you have to. If your **best friend** wants to help, but you know it won't work out, then say no. Just because someone is a **great friend** does not mean they will be a great business partner.

Let's Talk About Selling

Earlier you thought about how to make your idea unique and stand out. This is all part of selling it. You need to convince people that they *have* to have it. You need to catch their attention and make them want to learn more. Once you have "hooked" them, you can go on to add other details.

You might see your parents go buy a new computer or buy their first dishwasher. What you probably don't see is all the research they had to do before buying it. One thing they would have looked into was how long each brand lasts for. If one dishwasher brands claims theirs lasts for 5 years, but another one claims theirs lasts for 10 years, which one are you going to buy? You need to think of a life cycle for your product, be sure to be **honest and realistic.** How long do you think one of your products is usually going to last?

One detail you probably haven't learned about yet and will need a grown-up's help with, is making sure your idea hasn't already been claimed by someone else. Just because you haven't seen a **commercial** for it, doesn't mean someone else hasn't already thought of it. When a person thinks they have a great idea, they can try to get a patent for it. That means, they are buying the *idea*. So if you try to sell that product, even if you truly thought it was your idea first, you are not allowed because someone has a **patent**. There are other rules that are similar to this, but the bottom line is, have a grown-up help you research and make sure you are allowed to sell your idea.

Let's Talk About Money

Put a grown-up in charge. Honestly, there are so many factors to think about, that it is just a lot for a kid to handle, no matter how awesome you are. However, that is not to say you shouldn't try to learn about what's going on. And it definitely does not mean that you shouldn't check in.

Not only to do you want to make sure everything is going the way it should, but you also might need to change your plan. If you're not making as much as you thought, but you're spending a lot to make your product, then you need to change your thinking.

Sit with a grown-up and write down every expense there is to bringing your product or service to fruition. Now it is time to calculate how much money you will need to earn in order to sustain your business. This is very important and essential to understanding how to price your product or service. Having a great business is awesome, but having a profitable business is AMAZING! Be sure to set clear goals.

Keeping accurate records is important too. A grown-up can create and maintain a simple Excel worksheet of all of your financial data. This is important to the overall strength and financial stability of your company. You must know how and where your money is being spent.

Once you work on this simple aspect of financial budgeting and understand, expenses versus revenue, you and your support system can work on a long-term financial projections plan. This is more advanced than we will discuss in this book.

Let's Talk About Structure

You have been thinking about what kind of business you want and also about who should be the boss. Well, there are more choices than you might realize for planning out who is in charge and what everyone should be doing. A grown-up (parent/guardian) will have to set-up your business and sign the proper documents because you are a minor. Take a look at some of the most popular business set-ups to see what feels right for you:

- Sole proprietorship: This is a one-person business.

- Partnership: This is a business owned by two or more people.

- **Limited Risk Organization (LLC):** This is a good one for KiddiePreneurs, because it may seem complicated at first, but one person is not in charge, which helps to protect the **KiddiePreneur** from being the one blamed if there is ever a problem.

- **Cooperative:** This is a business where everyone is considered equal.

- **Non-profit:** This is a business where revenues are used to further the mission of the **organization** which are typically service oriented, **community focused.**

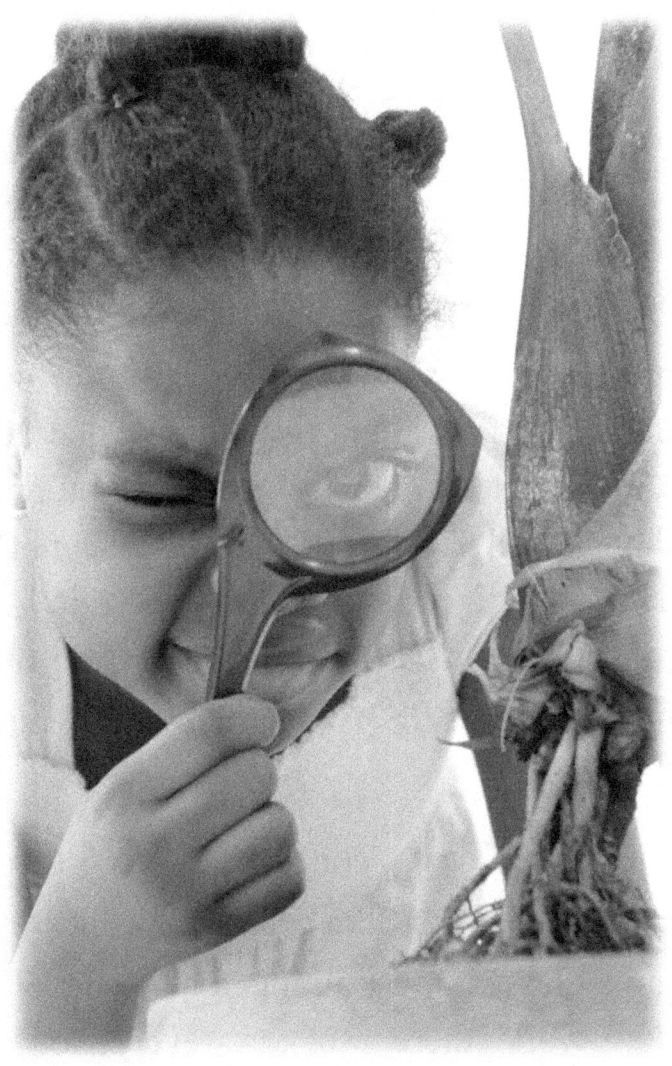

Let's Talk About Learning

As a **KiddiePreneur,** you need a lot of skills for your business to succeed. The **better your business** does, the more you are going to need to know so that it continues to grow. But how do you know what you need to learn, if you are doing it all for the first time? Fear not! This list will prompt you on where to go to get help in order to make sure you have all the **skills you need** to run your business.

Plus, you don't need to learn **everything alone!** Great businesses have classes and training for the people that work there, so that everyone is learning the **newest information.** Having training for everyone will motivate them and help improve your business. A lot of times in business you call this coaching. Grown-ups register your KiddiePreneurs in the awe-inspiring online kids-focused business classes offered through the KiddiePreneur Online Training Academy, which is online at www.KiddiePreneur.com. KiddiePreneurs will be able to network with other KiddiePreneurs nationwide and also have the remarkable opportunity to participate in the KiddiePreneur Online Training Academy graduation.

The Basics

As a **KiddiePreneur,** ease yourself into everything by starting with the basics. There are certain skills that are most **important for a beginner.** First, would be **leadership skills.** You need to feel comfortable being a leader and taking charge; otherwise the business is never going to go the way you planned. Second, you need to be a **hard worker.** It is probably quite obvious by now that starting your own business is not easy, and it takes a lot of hard work and dedication. Finally, you really need to become comfortable **taking risks.** It can be scary at first! And by no means do I think you should **jump at** any risk you could possibly take. **Think** about it first, but if the only thing holding you back from a big decision is fear that it is risky, then **take the risk!**

Step It Up

Once you have **mastered** the basics, then you can **start** to take on some of the **harder skills.** You passed the first round and are now on to round two!

- **Finance:** This is just a fancy word for money. Start to pay closer attention to where all the money goes and how to plan it all out.

- **Marketing:** This is a different way you can "sell" your product. Maybe you put out ads, hang flyers, give discounts, or simply hope the word gets spread around.

- **Sales:** This means learning about pricing, getting the best deals, helping customer and keeping track of the competition.

- **Personnel:** Think about how the word "person" is hiding inside the word "personnel." This is about the people - who you hire, who is a great worker, or could be teaching new workers.

- **Personal Business Skills:** This could cover many things, but start by getting yourself organized and learning how to use a computer and different computer programs. Always seek to increase your business knowledge.

The Expert

As your **business develops,** the skills your business needs to get to the next level will become more advanced as well. For example;

- As your **company** grows your finances will increase as well. You may need to hire an accountant to oversee your *company's finances.*

- Your *marketing* needs may need to change to adapt to the every changing environment.

- You may need to find a bigger location as *your business expands.*

- You may need new equipment to support your *expanding business.*

Let's Talk About Location

Picking a **business area** might be the most important choice a KiddiePreneur will make, so you need to plan and explore! Remember what you have learned about planning your neighborhood. If you want to open a make-your-own-jewelry shop, then don't open your store on the same street as another **jewelry store.** So think about the area, check out the competition, and watch your budget. Make sure you know how much you can afford to pay in rent or to have a **work space.**

What's great is that you are just starting up. There is a great **possibility** that you can operate your business from home. This, however, depends on your business needs and is completely at the discretion of your parent or guardian.

This will save the start-up company a lot of money, especially in the beginning.

Let's Talk More About Money

You are probably **wondering** how in the world you are supposed to find the money to start all of this. Well, it's complicated. There are a few different things you can try, but as a **KiddiePreneur** you are at a bit of a **disadvantage.** Banks won't give you money because you have no **business history** to prove you are **worth the risk.** This is the time when your **motivation** and determination really need **to kick in.**

Make your own KiddiePreneur business card. Grown-ups will "network" in the business world. This means, if they meet someone that they think could help their business, they hand them their business card and try to connect with that person. If you are out grocery shopping with a grown-up one day and there's someone talking on their phone while shopping about his or her company, take a KiddiePreneur business card out of your back pocket and hand it to them. Put on a brave smile and give them your *short mission statement* and say you are looking for people or companies to donate money to help get it started.

There is always fundraising, asking for donations, and just getting the word out. Maybe you can even have a grown-up help you call the local newspaper. Many times they look for stories about people in town and what they are trying to do. But whatever you do, don't give up!

Tag Team Approach

Parents your KiddiePreneur needs you too. Starting a business can be rewarding and fun, but some aspects may

be a bit challenging for a KiddiePreneur to navigate alone. Super parents to the rescue! Because your budding KiddiePreneur is likely to be under the age of 18, they will need you to help in the following areas as needed:

- **Signing all legal documents.** Remember parents, you are ultimately responsible for your child's business.

- **If you need major funding,** parents you can apply for loans to help out your KiddiePreneur.

- **KiddiePreneur** parents are responsible for reporting your KiddiePreneurs business income. Business tax laws vary per state. Research, research and research again to avoid any penalties!

- **Helping your KiddiePreneur** obtain an EIN, An Employer Identification Number (EIN) is also known as a Federal Tax Identification Number, and is used to identify a business entity. Generally, businesses need an EIN. You may apply for an EIN in various ways, including online.

- **Acquiring licenses** and permits as needed according to your jurisdiction.

- **Most importantly** they need your absolute support.

What's In A Name

So you've done a lot of work. Take a moment to stand up dance and give yourself a huge standing ovation. You are almost there!

Now that you have thoroughly examined your business idea, you need a business name. This is the fun part.

Think of a cool, creative, spunky business name that fits the products or services that you are selling. For example, let's say that you are selling sneakers. You can name your company various ways "Sneakz" "SneakerZ" "Dashing Footwear" etc. You get the point. Have fun thinking of a business name.

Once you have a few business names in mind, you want to research to ensure that the names are not taken or copy written by another company. The internet can be your friend in helping you in the research process. A search on the internet will help you out quite a bit, more specifically, search the U.S. Small Business Administration.

Successful KiddiePreneurs

While most kids stick with lemonade stands, some **young KiddiePreneurs** take their business much further. Millions of dollars and multiple countries later, kids have created products for technology, computers, business, and even bacon. Here are just some of the **KiddiePreneurs** already making a splash in the world!

Sean Belnick

Sean is now 34 years old, but started his business at 14. With just $500 and some **quiet space** in his bedroom, he created a design for a chair that turned into a full business. He founded

BizChair.com and now offers all sorts of furniture, from medical equipment to furniture for homes, schools and offices. Sean now has 75 people working for him and has sold supplies to American Idol, Microsoft and the Pentagon! Oh, and did I mention he made $24 million in the first five years?

Adam Horowitz

Adam Horowitz is the perfect example of how you should not give up just because you made a bad decision or made a mistake. When he was 15, Adam and some friends started a mean blog where they talked about other people. The parents shut it down quickly and Adam learned from that. However, he still liked how powerful the internet could be. So Adam came up with a new idea. He created a website called Urban Stomp, which had music and said where different parties were in the area. He raised money by selling clothes, but hit a bump in the road when he put the wrong address in for a party. About 700 teenagers showed up ready for some fun...to his 80-year-old neighbor's house. But did Adam give up? No!

Adam now teaches other kids about making money on the computer and is in charge of marketing sites like "Mobile Monopoly" and "Cell Phone Treasure." Both of those two sites have earned him more than $100,000. He also has a new site starting called "Dude, I Hate My Job!"

Leanna Archer

Leanna was only 13 years old when she got her big business idea. People were always asking her about her beautiful hair and what she did to make it so wonderful. Well, her grandma had a secret recipe for her own hair product that she would make herself. At first, when she came up with the idea of selling this, her parents were not happy. They were worried it would not be a good idea. But her grandma whipped up a batch for her and then Leanna stuck it into little jars to sell to her friends and her friends' parents. The money quickly started rolling in and now she owns "Leanna's Hair."

Abbey Fleck

Who doesn't love crispy, tasty bacon? Abbey was only 8 years old when she was helping her dad make bacon one morning. Usually, when you are cooking bacon, a lot of grease forms at the bottom of the pan. The grease isn't healthy, so you are supposed to drain it out or soak it up with a paper towel. Well, they were out of paper towels and needed to think of something quick. Both Abbey and her dad decided to let the grease drip off the bacon. That gave them the idea for finding a way to "drip cook" bacon all the time. Abbey and her dad created a dish you can put in the microwave with a deep dish below to collect the grease. After the bacon is done cooking, you just throw out the grease. Genius!

Business Ideas

So, you're **excited,** right? But...where do you begin? Maybe you already have an idea and are ready to be off and running. However, maybe you really want to **start a business,** but aren't sure what kind of business you should start. Here are a few ideas that are perfect for KiddiePreneurs.

- Entertaining at Kids' Birthday Parties
- Making Personalized Pet Tags
- Creating a Fruit Stand
- Making Candy Bar Arrangements
- Teaching Musical Instrument Lessons
- Starting a Rock Band
- Making Homemade Cards
- Making Lip Gloss or other Cosmetics

- Making Headbands
- Making Hair Scrunchies and Ponytail Holders
- Making Hair Bows and Flowers
- Making Friendship Bracelets
- Knitting Scarves
- Making Holiday Ornaments
- Making Decorated Tins
- Making Homemade Wrapping Paper
- Creating Scrapbooks or Memory Books
- Creating T-shirts

Well my little KiddiePreneurs, you have all the information you need to get started. Remember, if you really want this, never give up. Now off you go and start your business!

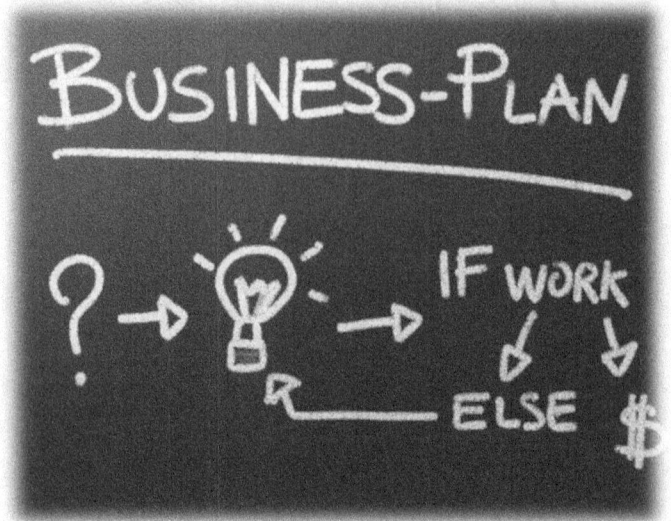